The Greatest Viking EVER

Written by

Tony Bradman

Illustrated by

Shahab Shamshirsaz

OXFORD

OXFORD
UNIVERSITY PRESS

Great Clarendon Street, Oxford, OX2 6DP, United Kingdom

Oxford University Press is a department of the University of Oxford.
It furthers the University's objective of excellence in research, scholarship,
and education by publishing worldwide. Oxford is a registered trade mark
of Oxford University Press in the UK and in certain other countries

Text © Tony Bradman 2015
Illustrations © Shahab Shamshirsaz 2015

First published 2015

British Library Cataloguing in Publication Data
Data available

ISBN: 978-0-19-835668-4

10 9 8 7 6 5 4 3 2 1

Paper used in the production of this book is a natural, recyclable product
made from wood grown in sustainable forests. The manufacturing process
conforms to the environmental regulations of the country of origin.

Printed in China by Hing Yip

Acknowledgements

Series Advisor: Nikki Gamble

There were once two brothers who lived on a farm in the land of the Vikings. Olaf was the younger one, and Ivar was the older one. They were very different.

This is the tale of what happened when they went on a voyage.

It all started when Ivar decided he was bored with being a farmer.

"I want to be a Viking and have amazing adventures!" he said. "In fact, I'm going to be the greatest Viking **ever**! Um, I'll need a crew to go to sea with me …"

Ivar rounded up his friends – Gudrun, Erik,
Snorri and Helga.

"That's still not enough," said Ivar. "You'll
have to be in my crew, too, Olaf."

"Oh no, not me," said Olaf. "I'm far too
busy here."

It was true, Olaf had plenty to do.
Somebody had to look after the farm.
Not that Olaf minded doing all the work –
unlike Ivar, Olaf loved being a farmer.

He particularly liked taking care of the
animals and they liked him, especially
the sheepdogs.

But Ivar simply wouldn't take no for an answer. "You're coming with us, Olaf, and that's the end of it," he said. "Now, we should prepare for our voyage. We'll need **helmets** and **shields** and ..."

"A ship might be useful," said Olaf.

"I knew that!" snapped Ivar. "Er ... I just hadn't got round to finding one yet ..."

So off they went in search of a ship.

They looked at **big** ships

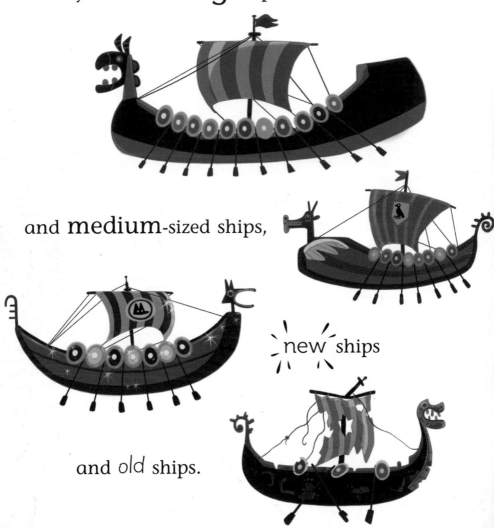

and **medium**-sized ships,

new ships

and old ships.

But there was only one that Ivar could afford.

"It will be fine," said Ivar, slapping the planks. His hand went straight through the side. There were other problems, too. The mast was a bit loose, the rigging was in a tangle, and there weren't enough oars.

"I name this ship *The Sea Snake*," declared Ivar.

"More like *The Sea Snail*," muttered Olaf. But he did his best to fix the ship.

They set sail on a bright, sunny morning.
But soon dark clouds filled the sky and a storm
came roaring from the north, tossing
the ship on huge waves.

"I feel terrible," groaned Ivar. Most of the others felt just as bad. Olaf was all right though and he steered *The Sea Snake* through the storm.

"I think we should head for the nearest land," said Olaf. Ivar's face had gone green and he couldn't speak. Olaf shrugged and changed their course.

They came at last to a land of
forests, rocks and mountains. Olaf dropped
the anchor and they all went ashore. Ivar
and the others were feeling better now.

"Right, let's go and have an adventure!" said Ivar. "Follow me!"

He set off towards the forest and most of the others went with him.

"Hang on a second," Olaf called out. "We've got no idea what's in there …"

"That's the point, isn't it?" said Ivar. "Come on, it will be great!"

Olaf sighed and trudged into the forest.

It was dark and spooky beneath the trees.
Owls hooted, bats swooped and a wolf howled
in the distance. Soon Ivar's hands were shaking
and his knees were knocking together.

"I can't see where the path goes,"
he moaned. "I think we're lost!"

Suddenly they heard a loud **THUD**.
And then several more: **THUD,**

THUD,

THUD.

The ground began to shake.
Something huge was coming
their way!

At last a giant troll burst out
of the trees – and grinned.

"I'd been wondering what
to have for lunch ..." she said.

Ivar screamed and tried to run away but the troll reached out and grabbed him. She licked her huge lips and slowly raised Ivar towards her enormous mouth. It was as wide as a cave.

"I wouldn't do that if I were you,"
said Olaf in a loud voice.
The troll paused and looked down.
"Really?" she said with a smirk.
"Why is that? Are you and your
little friends going to stop me?
Ooh, I'm so scared."

"You should be,"
said Olaf. "He won't
taste good – in fact,
he's poisonous."
The troll instantly
dropped Ivar.

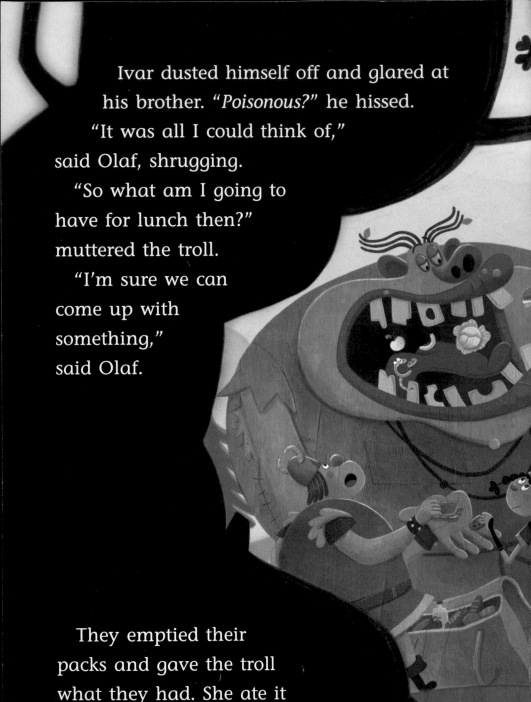

Ivar dusted himself off and glared at his brother. "*Poisonous?*" he hissed.

"It was all I could think of," said Olaf, shrugging.

"So what am I going to have for lunch then?" muttered the troll.

"I'm sure we can come up with something," said Olaf.

They emptied their packs and gave the troll what they had. She ate it

"Sorry about being so grumpy," she said. "I get like that when I'm hungry."

"No problem," said Olaf. "By the way, is there anything worth seeing up ahead?"

"Not much," said the troll.

"Er ... except for a fortress and some hidden treasure ..."

"Hey, now you're talking!" said Ivar, his eyes wide with excitement.

So they said goodbye to the troll and set off
down the path once more. It twisted and turned
through the trees and eventually led uphill.

At last they saw the grim fortress on a craggy
hilltop. The walls were tall and thick. There
were no guards and the gate was open.

I have a bad feeling about this," said Olaf.
"We should be careful ..."

"You worry too much," said Ivar. He went in.

There was a courtyard beyond the gate, with doors that led to a great hall. A fire was burning even though the hall was empty.

They searched for the hidden treasure but found nothing. Then Ivar spotted another door and opened it to reveal some stairs leading downwards.

"I'm sure this is where we'll find the treasure!" said Ivar as the crew descended. "It's a bit dark down here though, isn't it? We need a torch ..."

Olaf lit a torch – and their mouths fell open.

They found themselves in an **enormous** cellar full of treasure. It glittered in the flickering light of Olaf's torch – mounds of gold coins and jewels.

Ivar and the crew laughed and cheered. They dived into the treasure and threw it at each other. They swam in it and stuffed it in their pockets.

"Hold on, I should get the largest share," said Ivar. "Tell them, Olaf!"

But Olaf was peering into the shadows that his torch didn't reach.

Two burning red eyes were staring at him.

A gigantic wolf emerged
from the shadows and
growled, showing its teeth.

"I am Fenrir, Guardian of the Treasure,"
snarled the wolf. "Who are you?"

"I'm … I'm the greatest Viking of all time," said Ivar, holding up his shield and trying to sound brave. "And I've come to take the treasure, so there!"

"I don't think so," growled Fenrir. Then he **ROARED**, showing his razor-sharp teeth, and Ivar screamed. Fenrir chased the crew round and round the cellar, snapping at their heels.

Olaf gulped. But he knew what he had to do.

The beast was just a big dog really, and dogs always liked Olaf.

Olaf whistled – and Fenrir stopped in his tracks.

"Hey, boy!" said Olaf. "You must get pretty lonely and bored down here. Want to play?"

Fenrir stared at him with his burning red eyes ... then nodded eagerly.

Olaf threw things for Fenrir to fetch and then they played hide-and-seek.

"You're a big softie, aren't you?"
said Olaf, tickling Fenrir's tummy.
Fenrir wriggled happily.

Ivar, however, didn't look happy. In fact, he was totally miserable.

"I'm useless at being a Viking!" he groaned. "This voyage has been a disaster."

"What are you talking about, Ivar?" said Olaf. "We survived a great storm, defeated a troll and stood up to Fenrir! We're heroes, especially you!"

Ivar smiled. "I suppose we are," he said. "What shall we do now?"

"I think ... we'd better go home," said Olaf, and the crew agreed.

Fenrir was sad to see Olaf go, and insisted on giving him a little something ...

For a farm boy, Olaf had made a good
Viking. But he was glad to get home.

Ivar told everyone about their great adventure.
The story wasn't quite as Olaf remembered it ...
but he loved his brother so he didn't say a word.